# 20-Something & Rich

## A Step-by-Step Guide to get Rich and Build Wealth in Your Twenties and Beyond

---

Latasha Kinnard

20-Something & Rich

Copyright © 2013 by Latasha Kinnard

ISBN (978-1494429706)

Printed in USA

# DEDICATION

This book is dedicated first and foremost to my Lord and Savior Jesus Christ. I would also like to acknowledge my family for being so amazingly supportive of me. So thank you Christine Marshall, Duane Kinnard, Tenecia Kinnard, Shaniqua Kinnard, and Treveyon Kinnard. Your unconditional love has made this book possible. Lastly, thank you to the rest of my friends and family for your amazing support and encouragement.

# TABLE OF CONTENTS

Foreword ........................................ 6

Preface ......................................... 12

Introduction ................................... 19

Leaving a Legacy .......................... 29

Start with Strategy ....................... 52

Building a Budget ......................... 65

Demolishing Debt .......................... 83

Correcting Credit ......................... 103

Increasing Income ....................... 117

Quiz Answers ............................. 128

"He who loses money, loses much; He who loses a friend, loses much more; He who loses faith, loses all."

-Eleanor Roosevelt

# FOREWORD

I would like to welcome you as a reader to what I believe is a very timely and much needed book written for young adults. I am extremely pleased to introduce this book to you and share my thoughts as to why you should take the time to read this book on how to be rich in your 20's.

My name is Mark A. Wingo, author of *Wingonomics: How to Become a Cash Flow Millionaire on Any Budget, in Any Market*. I'm also the President and Chief Executive Officer of New Beginning Financial Group, LLC a Tax, Insurance and Financial Services Company. I've been in the financial service industry since 2001.

What makes me excited about this book is that my financial journey has been a rollercoaster ride. Aside from the fancy title and accomplishments, I've had my fair share of financial troubles, partly because I had absolutely no childhood foundation about money. I never learned how to make money, how to keep money or how to have my money work for me. So, when I entered adulthood in my 20s, I learned a few hard lessons.

The sad part of my story is that I was working in the financial industry. As I entered the financial industry on my own I made it my mission to learn how money really works and how to obtain wealth. It was a hard lesson. I only wish I read a book like this to help me avoid some financial mistakes along the way, invest my money and build a business. If you are looking to get an early edge on your financial future, this book was written specifically for you. Your 20s are critical if you want to create wealth. If you have the right mindset and financial approach to money management, business development and tax planning you can potentially have your money work for you.

I'll never forget when I met Latasha Kinnard. She was a short young woman that I looked down upon. And I mean no disrespect when I say I looked down on her. I literally had to look down! I stand a giant 6 foot 6 inches, and she stands 5 foot 2 inches. But don't let her height fool you. She has a big heart, an amazing vision and a tenacity that is unmatched. Plus, her faith is allowing her to stand tall and make a lot of noise with her passion of teaching young adults how to build wealth. During our meeting she told me her story and why she's excited to be teaching people about personal finance and how to create wealth. I was amazed by her story of how she, like me, overcame the inner city to pursue her dreams to eradicate the wealth gap and reduce poverty. Since I've known her she has put in the hard work to add value to the lives of her clients. She has helped them increase their cash flow, net-worth and self-worth. There are not many other financial educators who are focused on uplifting others as they pursue their own dreams. It is truly something to behold.

When Latasha told me she was writing a book for young adults in their 20s, I knew it was the right time. We live in a society where the financial industry does not educate young adults for what lies ahead after college. In addition to my lack of financial education as a child, I believe college was a moment where I was mislead about the importance of money. Although I received a college scholarship, I was still a victim to on campus credit card offers and student loans. Once out of college, despite my credit card debt, I felt it was time to purchase a home and a car. I had a debtor's mindset. If I had met someone like Latasha while in college or right after college to teach me about personal finance, I would have probably avoided debt, had more cash in my bank account and accelerated my wealth potential, all because of the proper financial guidance to lead me down the right path.

One of the main reasons this book has sparked my interest is that it is straight to the point with no fluff. Latasha has a "tell it like it is" approach. With her financial teachings she will point out your financial flaws and simultaneously inspire you to do better. You will learn to transform bad behaviors into positive habits that will allow you to create wealth. In order for this change to occur, Latasha's going to ask you to start at ground zero and establish a firm foundation. If you are up for the challenge I'm confident after reading this book you will be equipped with all of the resources and tools to create a game plan to achieve whatever financial goals you may have.

If you happen to visit her website you will see on her home page that she starts by asking those straight to the point questions:

- Do you stick to a budget?

- Do you have a 6-month emergency fund?

- Do you save at least $100 every month?

- Do you have any investments like stocks and bonds?

- Are you ready to start planning for financial success?

No matter how you answer these questions, you will find that this book will allow you to clearly map out your vision, encourage you take actions towards them and challenge you to dream big. To me, that is one of the most refreshing parts of Latasha's teachings. I'm a firm believer that there is no one size fits all approach to creating wealth. And Latasha understands that. She goes against the norm by telling you about the true ways wealth can be created, no matter what society tells you. She truly believes that if you have the desire to jumpstart your financial future and you're willing to put in the work, you will get results. But first, you have to understand the process.

After being in the industry for years, I know the road to create wealth is unpredictable and painful. Having said that, I know this book will open your eyes to the possibilities and get you on the right track. It will get you to answer those tough questions that everyone who wants to create wealth should be asking. I know after reading this book a lot of your financial question will be answered and your later financial years will be prosperous.

"An investment in knowledge pays the best interest."

- Benjamin Franklin

# PREFACE

When I was a little girl, maybe 9 years old, I would count the pennies in my mom's penny jar. She would never let me have them all, but I would often dip into the jar and spend a few dollars in pennies so that I could keep my real dollars in my pocket. Even then, it struck me how the forgotten penny could grow into something so substantial and useful.

In fact, I think those pennies were the seeds that sprouted my desire to get rich and build wealth at a young age. For the rest of this chapter I would like to tell you how a budding desire grew and blossomed into something much more tangible. Most personal finance books focus on facts and concepts, and this one will too. But before we begin, I want to delve quickly into the story of my life. One day, it will be a rags- to-riches tale, but for now I hope that it inspires you to hope for a better tomorrow.

Now, back to the story…

As my interest in money grew I began keeping a spending journal. By the time I was 11 I kept pretty accurate records of every single penny that came in and out of my proverbial piggy bank. For a youngster I was quite meticulous in my efforts. It was fun for me to keep track of my money and watch it grow. Every allowance, every birthday, and every Christmas I put a little bit away. I was so good at saving that my parents began to wonder how I had so much money.

Dollars turned into tens, and tens turned into hundreds. By the time I was in high school I had hundreds of dollars saved up under my mattress or in various other hiding spots. This was a huge accomplishment for me. A family friend, Lorraine, noticed my efforts, contributed to my stash of cash, and encouraged me to open up a bank account. A few days later, my mom accompanied to open my first savings account. I don't even think my parents had bank accounts at the time. With four kids to take care of their money was pretty tied up. In high school, I got my first job! I remember very vividly my granny telling me that from that point on, work would be a constant part of my life. Yikes! That was not comforting at all. I worked one day a week starting my junior year and by the time I went to college I had well over one thousand dollars in the bank. I thought I was a pretty big deal.

Imagine how it felt to be a young girl from the inner city (since it's not PC to say ghetto) who had managed to save $1000 dollars with birthday money and from working one day a week. Each step of the way I was learning how little actions could have a big impact. I was fascinated with how money worked and how it interacted with real life. It was weird to me that even though I had money in the bank I didn't really have much in real life. But if I spent the money I had in the bank, then I wouldn't have any at all. How baffling.

I grew up in a poor neighborhood on the South Side of Chicago. Many adults didn't work and considered "money" to be some form of government aid. Don't imagine that there is judgment in my tone. I have none to give. For several, that was all that they knew. They were on government assistance just like their mom and their mom's mom. Many find themselves trapped in a vicious cycle that is surely perpetuated by lack of knowledge. But I wanted to get out.

By the time I was a Junior I was investing in the stock market. At first I was scared, but hey, I had very little to lose and so much to gain. So I went for it. I didn't know what I was doing but since I knew how to read I trusted that I would be able to figure it out. I went to a website, took some test, and they recommended a few mutual funds. I picked one semi-randomly after reading an article called "How to pick the right mutual fund". As time went on I actually learned how to analyze investments while my own were just starting to bud. I started out with $50 per month, but just like everything else, it was a seed that would one day grow into much more.

When refund checks came I added money to my investments, when tax time came I added more money, and when my work-study checks came, I added even more. At this point, I had more money than I could have ever thought possible (which is sad because it was only a few thousand dollars) and I wanted to go further. I was beginning to develop a concept of financial freedom and considering how to build wealth so that it would not only impact my bank account, but also my lifestyle. And the bud flourished.

Upon graduation, I was recruited to work for a fortune 50 company. It was fabulous! I lived in a downtown sky rise apartment. I went out to parties, to dinner, theatre, and did anything else that I wanted. I had literally and figuratively "moved on up," but there was one little problem: I didn't love my job.

Some of you might be thinking, "cry me a river". This is the type of thing we call #firstworldproblems. I totally get it. But because of the decisions that I had made along the way I was in a position to dictate my life and my lifestyle. I did not have to whine or complain. My financial situation gave me the power to change my circumstances and the security to live with the consequences. I left corporate America, started my own business, and have been living happily ever since. My mission is to help my clients take control of their finances so that they can make their big dreams an even bigger reality.

My story is still building from this place of entrepreneurship. So far, it has been an amazing rollercoaster ride with momentous highs and excruciating lows, but I appreciate every minute of it. I hope I didn't bore you with the details of how I developed my relationship with money and how I started my path to wealth. But I want you to know that even with humble beginnings you can get on track to reaching your financial goals. I've been where you are. Whether you are in corporate America making more money than you ever have, or if you are just starting out with little to no direction, I've been there. And now, I just hired my first property manager to manage my new real estate portfolio. And life is good.

All you have to do is take hold of the things that are important to you and let that be your motivation. Looking back I can see that my journey began even before I knew it. And I'm sure yours did too. The reason I am writing this book is because financial freedom should not be just for the elite. It should be for everyone. It should be for you and me and our families and our communities. So let's make it happen.

"Opportunity is missed by most people because it is dressed in overalls and looks like work."

-Thomas Edison

# STEP-BY-STEP GUIDE

Building wealth is easy. You just have to know what you are doing. It is impossible to go into every single aspect of wealth building within the confines of one book, but we will cover many of the below.

1. Identify goals and priorities
2. Create a budget
3. Improve your credit score
4. Maximize your income
5. Decrease your spending
6. Pay down debt
7. Contribute to your 401k at least to the company match (low cost investments)
8. Open up and max out your IRA (low cost investments)
9. Get Insurance and Plan Estate
10. Buy an investment property instead of a home

# INTRODUCTION

In the preface I gave the charge to every single reader to "make it happen". What was your initial response when you read that? Did you glance over it as a formality or did your mind begin to populate with ideas in anticipation for the change that it is about to come. I guess I should tell you now that this is not a touchy feely self-help book. Get ready to take massive action toward reaching your financial goals. You are the CEO of your life and you should be running it like a business, at least in some ways. You can consider me your personal financial consultant dedicated to helping you organize, maximize, and just generally get it together (with love).

There are tons of books on the market about how to get rich and build wealth, yet so many people are still living below their financial potential. This means one of two things is happening. Either authors are not writing books that actually impact the lives of the readers; or, people are reading good material but not putting it into action. To hold up my end of the bargain I promise to produce highly usable and transformative content. Anybody who even looks at this book for long periods of time will be transformed. I'm kidding. But in all seriousness I don't take my job for granted. I am here to help you get clarity in your financial life so that you can get more of what you want and do more of what you love. But, even with all of my powers, I can't do it by myself. And that brings me to my next point.

There is absolutely zero doubt in my mind that you are capable of achieving financial freedom. However, I have to tell you that everyone is not going to make it. It won't be because you lacked the tools or resources. Those things are clearly outlined in the book. If you do not reach your goals, it will be because you did not do your part. At the end of every chapter there are very clear deliverables that you need to complete as well as a quiz to help you increase your financial IQ. If you follow the steps outlined in the book and complete the deliverables, you will have a clear idea of how to turn your financial dreams into a financial reality.

I'm here to help you as much as I can. In fact, I hope that those of you who want to accelerate your path to wealth will consider becoming a client. At the very least, go to facebook and join the "20-Something & Rich" group page. This way, you can stay engaged with people who are working toward similar goals. But no matter how much I do, whether or not you reach your goals will depend on what you do and the choices you make. If you need an accountability partner, go find one on the facebook group. Accountability makes a huge difference. Opportunity is knocking right now. All of you are smart enough to open the door. That's what you did when you purchased this book. But not everyone is bold enough to walk through it and do what it takes to succeed. Are you one of the few who will commit to reading every chapter and doing every exercise? Only you can decide.

The art of decision-making can be tricky business. When you think about it, we are faced with hundreds of decisions every day. You must decide when you are going to get out of bed, what you are going to wear for the day, whether or not you are going to eat breakfast, which route will help you avoid traffic, what you will eat for lunch, whether or not you should watch that last episode of Law and Order (do it! No, don't!), and a host of other things. So it is clear that on some level most of us know how to make a decision.

Then why is it that we freeze up when it comes to making the decisions that really matter? Why do we stare at the fork in the road with days, weeks, and even years of inactivity. I wonder how many people are NOT reading these words right now because their book is tucked away securely on a bookshelf, or in the queue of an e-reader. If you really pull down the mask and honestly assess what is getting in the way of you and your decision to achieve financial freedom, I know that we would find a host of excuses packaged as reasons. But the time for excuses has abruptly come to an end. Like, now. When you picked up this book, you effectively made the decision that it was time to start achieving your financial goals. And don't mind my tone. Sometimes you might hear me come through as harsh or pushy. Just think of it as tough love. The odds are not in our favor so we have to work double time to reach our financial goals. I want to help you do that.

Right now, get over whatever you need to get over and make the decision to relentlessly pursue financial freedom. Some books about personal finance dedicate a full chapter to helping you develop the right mindset. It's that important. I truly believe that you will manifest those things that you think about the most; therefore, maintaining a positive outlook when it comes to money is absolutely critical to changing your financial situation. That being said, I have reduced the therapy session to one sentence: Get. Over. It. I know it's not that easy, and that it will take time to overcome financial baggage. That's fine. What I am saying is make the decision to not take no for an answer. You can do it. You have what it takes to become a millionaire, a multi-millionaire, or... gasp... a billionaire! Is there even a limit? I don't think so. But remember that the activity that you put into your finances will reflect what you get out. Now is the time to commit to massive and consistent action with your first step being to get through this book.

You may have noticed that even though I'm writing a book and I don't have the pleasure of speaking with you directly, in my mind, I envision that YOU are right here sitting across from me ready to receive and challenge everything that I have to say. Have you ever had a conversation with yourself? Well, as I'm writing, I am having a conversation with myself as if I am you. For example, sometimes you say things like, "But Tasha, everyone does not have the money that it takes to reach their financial goals." And when you do, I take it to heart, and think up a response (I bet you talk to yourself too sometimes). There are so many people out there who have tried year after year and have made resolution after resolution and are looking to make a real change that will lead to financial freedom. Well, I can't tell you that I have a magic bullet. But I do have access to experiences and information that I think you will be able to connect with. I try to make it so easy and simple that every person who sits across from me and every person that reads this book can implement strategies that will change your life.

The best part is that this stuff is not rocket science. But the inability to make decisions has left this information in a black box. So now, I am opening that black box, shattering your fear, and bringing to light all of the insecurities that you have had about money, and answering your insecurities with truth and information. Knowledge by itself is not power. But knowledge that can inspire action will change how you interact with money.

It is my goal that as you decide to do better with money, I will provide you with the tools you need to change your mindset, learn the information, learn how to do it, and then actually put it into action. This is not just about reading and learning. It is also about doing. 20-Something and Rich is a book that is about making inaccessible financial topics easy to understand. Managing money can be like taming a wild beast but it is absolutely worth the effort. In theory, personal finance should be simple, but the execution is difficult. Unfortunately, we often lack the knowledge, tools, and resources we need to make informed financial decisions that will guide us toward a path of financial freedom. Even though it is not given the respect it deserves, financial literacy is important to everyone's personal survival.

Lack of exposure to critical money management concepts leaves us vulnerable to financial failure. In the experiences that I have had thus far, money is still a taboo subject and is not something that we discuss openly. The majority of high schools, colleges, and universities, do not have financial literacy education and parents are not usually informed enough to pass on useful advice to their children. But, in the information age we are free to seek out the knowledge we need. Knowledge unlocks the door to financial freedom, and your own actions and decisions will put it within your reach.

I know from personal experience that this process can be quite the whirlwind. And with that being said, I must warn you to prepare yourself to do some work. In fact, we will be going hard and digging deep to create a plan that viably leads to financial freedom. I know that many of you have been setting goals and new years resolutions for years but to no avail. Well, setting a goal by itself is not enough to help you achieve anything. In fact, nothing can be achieved where knowledge is lacking. I think that sometimes we can forget that there is an "L" before earn. Meaning that if you want to be a top earner, you have to be a top learner!! Knowledge gives you the key, and action unlocks the door to financial freedom. So, in this book we are going to go in depth into the most important information that you will need to know in order to become a millionaire or simply to attain financial freedom.

In this book, we are going to talk about leaving a legacy, starting with a strategy, building the right budget, digging out of debt, correcting your credit, and increasing your annual income. We are going to talk about what you need to do now so that you can live the rest of your life like most people only dream about. I will introduce you to the most important financial concepts while motivating you to complete the tasks. If you are like me, thought based exercises can be annoying because the immediate benefits are hard to comprehend. But don't be a know-it-all. Nobody likes a know-it-all! Sometimes, you have to understand the situation before jumping head first into the solution.

I wrote this book especially for you. This is my first time ever putting my financial principals in a book that can be consumed on a large scale and I am sure that it is not perfect. I still have so much to learn. I have done my best to summarize the knowledge that I have gained over the years and condense it into a format that is relatable and easy to understand. Sometimes I rant and sometimes my passion gets the best of me. But I know that you will walk away with important nuggets, concepts and wisdom that will ignite a financial fire and accelerate your path to wealth. I'm excited for you, and I'm honored to come along for the journey as you work to achieve financial freedom in your twenties and beyond!

"I made my money the old-fashioned way. I was very nice to a wealthy relative right before he died"

-Malcolm Forbes

# Chapter 1:

# LEAVING A LEGACY

As young adults, it can be difficult to think beyond the here and now. The word "legacy" hardly even enters into our worldview unless it is about someone else's. This is the time where we are encouraged to enjoy life (even to the point of selfishness) in preparation for the many sacrifices that are to come. One day our list of responsibilities will multiply and our freedom will leave us. We might even have little people that share our DNA looking at us with big eyes and needing food, shelter, time, and affection.

As new experiences draw us deeper into adulthood, we become an important fixture that people depend on. Where before we only had to think of ourselves and could count on others to help support us, we now become the force that is helping to support others, whether it is a spouse, children, or parents. For some, this time has already come, but for many of us we are using our twenties as a time of fun and self-exploration without giving too much thought to how our actions will impact the future. But what if we were more purposeful and intentional with this time? What if we could expand our thinking to extend beyond ourselves and the moment? If we could do this, I think that we could change the world.

According to an article by professor William Domhoff from University of California, Santa Cruz, I am inclined to believe that the world is in need of change (no pun intended) especially regarding wealth distribution. In his article, "Wealth, Income, and Power", Domhoff explains that the top 1% owns 65% of financial securities and 61% of business equity. It is no surprise that wealth is highly concentrated at the top, we all know this. But it is scary to think that the problem is becoming even more pervasive. With every generation, middle class families are getting poorer and poorer and no one seems to notice. Let's not even talk about the impoverished. And let's really not talk about the implications about power because this book would get real academic real quick, perhaps even political. But that is not my purpose. I am primarily concerned with what this means for you and how it impacts your ability to achieve financial freedom and create a legacy that will impact your families for generations to come.

In the 14th century the word legacy was defined as "a *body of persons* sent on a mission." Unlike our present day concept, it represented a group of people who were trying to accomplish a common goal. It is derived from the Old French word *legatie* and the Latin *legatia*, meaning "ambassador" or someone who promotes a specific idea or activity. Before you start rolling your eyes because I just tried to get real deep by using French and Latin word etymology in a book about personal finance (and I used the word "etymology"), I had to go there. These interpretations bring to the forefront 3 factors that I believe have been lost from our common understanding of the word. However, they are extremely important in informing your concept of what it means to leave a legacy.

First, a legacy is not about one person. It is about a group of people who are working together for a common purpose. Today, the word is typically associated with a single person whose accomplishments or actions have impacted many. Our current understanding aligns with our cultural values of independence and self-reliance but seems to slightly differ from the original meaning of the word. Second, a legacy is not about being remembered. It is about accomplishing a specific mission. This designation is important because it shifts the definition from inspiring hopes, dreams, and ambitions to actually inspiring the actions behind them. Legacy then, is not really about the memory, but about action that leads to a specific result. Finally, building a legacy involves taking a stand and promoting what you believe in. This implies a passion that is so strong, you have to share it with everyone. Within the context of this chapter and this book, these concepts will prove to be useful in creating the framework for a financial legacy that merges our current definition with the added insight of collaboration and action.

The Millennial generation has a bad reputation. In his article, "Who are the Millennials?" Douglas Main says that we are "more civically and politically disengaged, more focused on materialistic values, and less concerned about helping the larger community." Apparently, we are more preoccupied with "money, fame and image." Douglas is not alone in his opinions. I have seen many such caricatures of the millennial generation plastered all over the Internet with different data points to support the arguments. I am sure that there is some truth to this, but I must loudly acknowledge that my experiences with young adults have allowed for a much more charitable interpretation of their general character (but I admit that I might be a bit biased).

It is true that most 20-Somethings of today want what we want when we want it. I am no expert, but I think this is just a situation of life imitating "art". Everything around us from our phones to the Internet tells us that we can get things quickly and fairly easily. But don't misunderstand our love for nice things, ease, and efficiency with a lack of morals or motivation. Most of us will work if we have to and give when we have to.

All of my clients are very hard working and as a rough estimate, I would say that about 60% of them give money to their families even at the expense of their own financial situation. When I first encountered this behavior I was surprised. I thought most people my age were selfish, but it turns out that we're not that selfish after all. Instead of saving more money toward retirement or future goals, several 20-Somethings insist on sending home large monthly allowances and making charitable contributions; sometimes, even against my counsel. With these experiences in mind, I began to wonder what would happen if young adults learned early on how to build wealth. How could they impact the people and causes that they care so much about? As one of the most educated generation in history (according INC magazine) I think that we could do great things to make our future even brighter. And our children's, and our grandchildren's, and our parents, and our neighbor's...you get the picture. I think we can do great things.

I decided to start your wealth journey with consideration for your future just to give you some motivation. It is easy to conceptualize the accumulation of wealth as an individual endeavor, but I would encourage you to expand your mindset. Building wealth is not just about you. Actually, the implications extend far beyond your own environment. Prosperity is transferred from generation to generation and the wealth of the 1% is growing even while the wealth of the 99% is shrinking. So, while the concepts of building wealth are fairly benign and simple, the implications are pretty drastic and revolutionary. When considered within this context achieving financial freedom does not only put money in your pocket, but it also defies the status quo. It might seem like this is just about your money and your quality of life, but you are part of a larger world. The decisions that you make will impact you, your family, and your community for decades to come. Every decision creates a ripple affect that extends further and longer than you might have imagined. Through your financial decisions you can choose to be an asset to your team, or you can choose to be a liability. But know that you are working within a system that is much larger than just you.

America has the largest wealth disparity in the developed world and we still have big companies like Wal-Mart who make gazillions of dollars but refuse to pay their workers a living wage. I really don't care how much money Wal-Mart makes. I love it when companies do well because I know that I can do that too one day. However, I do care when a company threatens the livelihood of their workers by not paying them enough. But I'm not here to bash Wal-Mart. I only tell you this so that you can consider your role in the financial ecosystem. Where do you fall on the food chain currently? In order to leave a legacy you need to position yourself differently, think differently, and start doing things differently. Wal-Mart and other companies do not care about helping you build wealth, a legacy, or anything else. This is why it is so important young adults are more thoughtful about their finances from the very beginning. I am keenly aware that the odds are not in our favor (I just saw Hunger Games) and the only way to change that is to leverage our time, which should be our most valued and sacred possession. We often act as if the decisions we make in our twenties don't really count. We feel that we have the rest of our lives to be responsible and make good choices. We use our twenties for fun and exploration reducing any bad decisions to "learning experiences". And who would take away your God given right to learn from your mistakes?

Well, the thing is, you really can't afford to make too many financial mistakes. I don't mean to be a Debbie downer but with the economic climate that we live in, any missteps are sure to have consequences that may not be evident now, but will certainly present themselves later. The truth is, our twenties are our greatest asset, and what a beautiful asset it is. The sooner we realize that, the sooner we can start changing things. I am not saying that you shouldn't have fun, but since when did fun become about spending money instead of enjoying life experiences with friends and family. Instead of choosing meaningful experiences we choose to lease a newer car over buying an older one. We choose to live by ourselves right out of college instead of getting a roommate. We choose to live the life we want now, instead of preparing for our own future or for the futures of those that will come after us. I am not pointing any fingers because I am guilty too. The reality is that we have no one in our corner urging us to do better. But now, you do.

## It Starts With You

Unfortunately, with little to no personal finance education in our schools our financial literacy is lacking. Most of us have never been taught how to properly manage money and yet, we are pushed into the real world and expected to fly. Instead, many young adults leave the nest and take a nosedive only to regain stability after stumbling through mistakes and poor decisions. In the beginning we take on copious amounts of credit card debt, we leave money on the table by not investing in our 401K, and we never get around to opening that IRA that we've heard so much about. We focus more on what is happening today instead of considering the many tomorrows that are likely to come.

Our generation has warmly accepted the term YOLO and all that comes with it. You probably know what YOLO means but just in case you don't it is an acronym that means you only live once. Somehow, this phrase has wrongfully become the poster child for poor decision-making and is often cited as a reason to enjoy the moment despite future consequences. YOLO is Carpe Diem for idiots. To quote a reputable source, Urbandictionary.com says YOLO is "The dumbass's excuse for something stupid that they did." And that sums it up rather nicely. But as you think about building your own wealth and leaving a legacy that strengthens your lineage, you simply cannot take on this perspective. You will need to ignore all the foolishness and mentally prepare for the discipline and sacrifice that it will take to achieve financial freedom.

You are entering into new territory. You are a trailblazer, an originator, and a first generation wealth builder. You are establishing a foundation with roots that go so deep they will impact your family for generations to come. This is what it means to leave a legacy. Does this sound intimidating to you? It should. Do you believe that you could be the one to usher in an era of prosperity for yourself and your loved ones? You should. It will be hard but it is absolutely possible. If you choose to take on the challenge of becoming a first generation wealth builder you will find yourself on a most beautiful journey. Know, and rest assured, that you can absolutely reach your goal. According to *The Millionaire Next Door*, 80% of millionaires are "first generation affluent". If they can do it, I am confident that you can do it too. You just have to make the choice and then follow through.

## Money Mindset

To become a first generation wealth builder or to advance your family's estate beyond it's current assets you will need to develop a strong and unwavering mental framework around money. You've probably noticed online articles titled something like "10 Things Wealthy People Do Differently" that highlight the fact that wealthy people think about money differently from the rest of us. For better or worse, my experience has taught me that this is true. Wealthy people do think about money differently. Overall, they have a positive view of money and they like it enough to keep it around.

You might be surprised to learn that a lot of people don't like money. Instead of keeping it to build wealth for themselves, most people give it away to build wealth for someone else. Every time that you buy something as a consumer, you are taking money out of your own pocket and putting it into someone else's. No one really thinks about it like this. A positive money mindset starts with an understanding of how money really works and continues to broaden your perspective about the many possibilities. Your mindset has the potential to bring wealth into your life or to push wealth out of your life, and it is largely dependent on your financial narrative.

Your financial narrative is shaped by your life experiences. To really understand the story you tell yourself about money you have to understand how your life experiences have impacted your financial outlook. As a young girl, my family never had my much money. Money was used as a resource to get the things that we needed, but rarely to get the things that we wanted. As the oldest of three siblings I was always concerned with not being a burden and helping to support my family. As an adult, I look at some of my actions and I am keenly aware of how they have been shaped by childhood. I am a big saver because I fear one day falling back into poverty. Sometimes I feel guilty whenever I buy something that is a "want" instead of a "need". I am extremely generous because I know what it feels like to have the generosity of others.

My experiences have allowed me to save, invest, and give, but they have also caused me to think about money from a narrow-minded position of lack instead of from a place of abundance. What has your own childhood taught you about money? What financial values and ideas have your parents instilled in you as a young child? How have they manifested themselves into your day-to-day thoughts and actions? As an ardent lover of Jesus, I also had to worry about my spiritual mindset about money. The bible does say that "the love of money is the root to all evil," but it also says that Christ came so that we might "have an abundant life." For some people, this can be confusing. Until you unpack these thoughts and ideas that impact your view, you will not be able to fully welcome prosperity into your life.

To better understand where you are currently, ask yourself these questions and gauge your response.

- Why do you I money?

- Is money good or bad

- What do I value? → comfort → service | friends & family | time off to experience new places

- Will money change me?

- What am I willing to do to get money? → work FT → housesit

- What will I never do for money?

- Why am I building wealth?

- Is it better to give or to receive?

- Are the wealthy entitled to help others?

- Am I good at saving money?

- What does financial freedom mean to me?

- Do I enjoy planning for my financial future or do I dread it?

- Do I like talking about money?

- Am I confident in my ability to make money?

- If I lost everything I had could I get it back again?

I am not going to ask you to write down your answers to these questions because I know you probably won't. I also will not give you the answers because there is not just one way to think about money. Develop your own mindset that is guided by your character. Just keep in mind that money is never intrinsically good or bad. It simply depends on the person who is using it.

## Expand Your Knowledge

Learning basic financial principles will give you part of the arsenal you will need to build wealth. Based on my academic research, personal experiences, and client interviews, I am convinced that the wealth gap is not primarily caused by a gap in income, but in knowledge. A study presented by business week confirmed my suspicions that Americans lack the basic financial skills that would enable them to build wealth. On May 30th, 2013, Bloomberg Business Week presented a study that was conducted by FINRA, a prominent financial regulatory organization. FINRA issued a 5-question multiple-choice quiz with extremely basic personal finance questions and asked people to answer them. The results were not shocking. Out of 25,000 adults only 14% could answer all of the questions correctly.

Increasing your knowledge about important financial topics will give you the tools you need to make better financial decisions. Even if nothing about your financial situation changes, simply increasing your knowledge can help you keep more of your hard earned money in your pocket. Understanding these principals will not only affect you, but will also begin to inform the financial narratives of your children and eventually their children. But in order to create this ripple effect, you will have to do more than just learn. You will have to execute these theoretical principals and apply them to your own life. That's when things really get real.

## It Takes a Village

I come to you with a real "started from the bottom" story and I am still building my empire as I write this. I have watched my investments double and triple, I have acquired valuable assets, and I have learned to successfully take on risk. I am student of money. I study the strategies of the wealthy and I pay close attention to what works. From my personal experience I can tell you that building wealth on your own is hard.

In order to get anything worth having, there are going to be challenges. Consider Steve Jobs and how much he sacrificed to achieve his current level of notoriety. There was a period where Jobs barely had money for food and would seek out free meals. He often couch surfed, staying with different friends because he had no place of his own to call home. The only reason he was able to make it is because of those friends who supported him as he was tinkering with computers. If you want to increase your chances of building wealth, you must have a support system that is deeply committed to your journey. You need to be around people who believe that if you win, they win too, and vice versa. These relationships are not commonly found in our independent, self-reliant culture. Our society values independence instead of co-dependence but I strongly believe that by leveraging a co-dependant financial relationship for 1-3 years you can dramatically accelerate your path to wealth. Let's take a look at some examples that I have encountered.

*Example 1:*

You and your best friend are single moms. Right now you both are paying rent, utilities, and other bills. Instead of continuing in this fashion you decide to move in together and cut your bills in half. The arrangement is not easy but you stick it out for two years. By the end of this time period both of you have saved toward a 6-month emergency fund, paid down debt, and have built a solid financial foundation that will allow you to more easily and securely work toward financial freedom.

*Example 2:*

You have just graduated and ended up taking a job at home. Your parents are nearing retirement and are really excited to have you back in the city. Instead of getting your own apartment you decide to move in with your parents. The $1000 that would have normally gone to a landlord can now go towards you and your parents. You kindly pay your parents $400 and use the rest to pay down your student loan debt and build an emergency fund. Your parents use the extra $400 toward their retirement account and everyone is happy.

*Example 3:*

You have just graduated from college and decided to take a job in a new city. You have a friend who lives in the city so you decide to be roommates. By reducing your rent you are able to save up for your emergency fund, which came in handy when your car broke down and you needed to buy a new one.

These are just a few examples demonstrating how you can leverage your relationships to build wealth faster. Now that you know all of these definitions, theories, and ideas about why your legacy is important, let us end this chapter with some practical next steps in the form a financial legacy toolbox.

## Financial Legacy Toolbox

### 1. Run Your Family Like a Business

Think of your family like a business with income, expenses, assets, and liabilities. Eventually, you will not be able to run the business and will be forced to pass it on to a successor. During your presidency, you must create the framework that will empower future generations to carry on a tradition of wealth. To do this, keep track of your financial assets, establish monthly financial meetings, and identify partners and successors.

### 2. Set up an Estate

Your estate includes everything that you own. When you die, everything that you do not take with you must go somewhere. Your estate begins to detail your succession plan. This includes but is not limited to:

- Your beliefs and values
- A guardian in the event of minor heirs
- A will
- A trust
- Tax considerations
- Education allowances
- Life insurance

3. Create a Will

If you are of age and sound mind and you have possessions, then you are legally able to create a will. Your will should include your name, a clear succession of assets to specific individuals, and a date and signature. Get the document notarized and on file and abide by your states' witness requirements so that it will have legal standing in probate.

4. Get Life Insurance

Life insurance offers life and death benefits that can create wealth or conserve wealth. Most young adults are skeptical because life insurance representatives can be quite pushy and annoying. But the truth is, all of us will die one day. Life insurance gives you peace of mind that your dependents will be well cared for in the event of your death. It also does so many other savvy things, but we will keep it simple by discussing the most basic forms.

*Term Insurance:*

As the name suggests, this type of insurance is for a specific term meaning that it has a beginning and an end date. If you die within those dates, then a beneficiary is able to collect. If you die outside of those dates you are not covered under the plan. This type of insurance is much cheaper, but it will eventually run out. And there is only a death benefit. When your term runs out you will likely need to get additional insurance and it will be much more costly. It can be useful when you are on a tight budget and you have dependents you need to look out for.

*Whole Life:*

This form of insurance covers you for your entire life, as long as you have been making regular payments. The policy will accrue cash value that you can use for different life events as if you were your own personal bank. The cash value is not much, but it can be considered as the more conservative part of your portfolio. Whole life policies are a great addition as long as you can afford to make the monthly payments for...your WHOLE LIFE. If you can do that, you will indeed be a winner. If not, you will have wasted your money. This policy has both life and death benefits and is in my opinion one of the ways the rich get richer.

Hopefully, after reading this chapter you will get excited about building your legacy as a first generation wealth builder, or even a wealth expander. By thinking beyond yourself it my hope that you understand how important this is and that you are part of a larger picture.

# RECAP

This chapter focuses on building a lasting legacy as a first generation wealth builder.

☐ **Legacy**
Not just about one person. It is about a group of people working together for a common purpose.

☐ **First Generation Wealth Builder**
You are embarking on a new journey and acting as trailblazer in a revolutionary setting. Get ready for the challenge.

☐ **Start Now**
Time is your most valuable asset so do not waste it. Use it wisely.

☐ **Money Mindset**
Having the right mindset will help keep you grounded while guiding you toward your financial goals. Don't forget who you are.

☐ **It Takes a Village**
Don't try to do it alone. It's hard enough as it is.

# QUIZ

1. In this chapter the word legacy is NOT described as...

    A. An ambassador
    B. A group of people working toward a mission
    C. The accomplishments of a single person

2. To create a will you must:

    A. Have significant assets
    B. Be of sound mind
    C. Have more than one beneficiary

3. Term insurance is:

    A. Attached to a specific presidential term
    B. Only valid for specific period of time
    C. Can be extended without going to the doctor

4. The older you are:

    A. The less expensive your life insurance
    B. The more expensive your life insurance
    C. Life insurance is not based on age

5. If you do not have a will:

    A. Your wife will get the majority of your estate
    B. Your assets will be frozen indefinitely
    C. Your estate will go to probate court

# DELIVERABLE

Take 20 minutes to write your final will and testament. It should include a list of possessions and/or assets that you would like to pass on to your loved ones.

_____

_____

_____

_____

_____

_____

_____

_____

_____

_____

_____

_____

_____

_____

"My formula for success
is rise early, work late
and strike oil."

-JP Getty

# Chapter 2:

# START WITH STRATEGY

Before you do a complete overhaul of your personal finances it is a good idea to start with a game plan. Otherwise, you are setting yourself up for failure. When it comes to making life changes we are often compelled by an emotional reaction that drives us to take drastic measures. But if these measures are not rooted in a realistic plan then all efforts will eventually fizzle out and die. Emotions by themselves are not executable, which is why so many New Year's resolutions die before the first 30 days. Instead of being moved solely by your emotional desire to change, let's throw some logic into the mix to create a strategy that will allow you to be successful.

Planning your own finances can be a lot like pulling your own teeth. People usually try to avoid it! Having a step-by-step guide might make it less intimidating, but it does not make it easy. To make this process as painless as possible this chapter outlines exactly what you need to do to develop a financial plan that will work for you. We will focus on planning areas of your financial life that matter the most including spending, saving, and investing.

Having specific goals will bring much needed clarity to your financial situation. Shining a light on your money management strategies can help expose issues that you never even knew were there. One problem that I find to be common is that young adults (and probably everyone else too) will often have one financial plan in their mind, but they are actually executing another. In other words, their actions do not line up with their mental goals. For example, John might tell me that buying a house is in the next three years is one of his top priorities. To confirm, I reference John's bank statements and consult his budget only to find that he is spending hundreds of dollars eating out every month, with ZERO dollars going toward a down payment for a home.

At this point, I explain to John that there is no down payment fairy (although there is sometimes down payment assistance) that is going to cover the down payment for him and that if he is serious about his goal of homeownership, he is going to have to have to buckle down and reallocate his spending. This reality check moment leaves John with a blank stare for at least one minute as he contemplates what he needs to do to get his life together. You might think that situations like this are an anomaly. Surely if John had half a brain he would know that having a down payment comes before homeownership. Well, yeah he does. But somehow, this stuff gets lost in translation and never becomes action. In some form or another 100% of my clients struggle with financial alignment, which can have serious emotional consequences.

Financial alignment connects your goals and actions to your internal value system. In chapter one we discussed that it was important to understand what you value. When your values are properly transferred into financial goals you will feel a sense of satisfaction from taking the action necessary to reach those goals. In other words values lead to goals and goals lead to action. When your actions are disconnected from your values and goals you will find that nothing will satisfy you. People who are out of financial alignment wonder why they are unhappy or why they feel so empty despite their financial success. Money by itself will not make you happy. Remember that it is just a tool that we use to get the things that we want in life. If you don't really know what you want in life, spending alone will not help you figure that out. So even as you acquire more things, the feelings of emptiness will remain. Trying to fill this void with material possessions will only leave you frustrated and broke. Addressing the root cause will require you to tap into your internal value system and use your money in ways that will make you happy.

If you are not yet convinced that you need a comprehensive financial strategy to be successful as a first generation wealth builder, don't worry because I am not done convincing you. Another reason that you need to have a game plan from the very beginning is because it will help you stay on track. The habits that you have developed up until this point were not developed overnight and they will not be undone overnight either. They are deeply rooted in your psychological make-up and cannot be overcome without some calculated measures. Having a strategy will help you make decisions that are inline with your new plan rather than reverting back to your old ways of doing things. And let's face it, we live in an ADD world where we can barely finish an email without checking Facebook. Your financial game plan will help you stay focused when something else momentarily pulls your attention away.

A successful personal finance strategy is built on a well-defined internal value system. These values are used to create S.M.A.R.T goals that are specific, measurable, attainable, relevant, and time-bound. Also, you need a process that is designed to meet your needs and will help you reach your S.M.A.R.T goals. This process should include regular planning, consistent tracking, and full automation. After you have done all of that, consider working with a professional or a great accountability partner that can help you operate at a level that will accelerate your path to wealth. Below are some recommendations that will help you get your strategy going in the right direction.

## Schedule a Monthly Update

If you want to give your finances the proper TLC, schedule a 30-minute update on the first day of every month. In this meeting you should take a look at your net worth, debt, savings, investing, and your future goals. In addition, you can take advantage of this time to take a look at your budget for the upcoming month. And if you really want to go the extra mile and plan like a business, consider your 3-month forecast.

Do you have any upcoming events that you should start planning for now? Upcoming events might include birthdays, Christmas, tax time, or anything else that requires upfront planning. All of these things should be considered in your monthly update.

## Plan to Budget Weekly

In addition to monthly planning it is also a good idea to plan at the week level, but this time we only need to focus on the budget. This is real life and things change quickly. Managing your budget monthly allows you to adjust to life so that you can stick as closely as possible to the budget that you created. If you wait until the end of the month to track your financial progress, it is very likely that you will have gone over your budget. And while I am sure that you will promise never to do it again, I am equally sure that you will...unless you do something different. By looking at your budget every week, you gain additional control over how you are spending your money. It also gives you more opportunities to adjust your spending so that you can stay on track.

## Check Your Main Account Daily

We live in a consumer driven economy that encourages us to spend, spend, spend. Take two minutes during your morning commute to take a look at your main spending accountant. This quick check-in helps to keep your money top of mind, gives you a realistic picture of your financial situation, and helps to motivate you toward your financial goals.

Keep in mind that money management is never a one size fits all type of thing. These are just a few examples of what you can do to start managing your finances more actively. What works for one person may not work for the next. But no matter what, having a specific strategy that is focused on results is better than not having a strategy. To summarize, start with your values, (S.M.A.R.T) goals, and actions. Then, create a consistent process that will help you make your goals become a reality. Most people have trouble sticking to these strategies because they bite off more than they can chew. Start small and watch as small changes impact your life in a big way.

# RECAP

This chapter focuses on creating a strategy that will allow you to reach your financial goals.

☐ **Strategy**
Without a strategy you are setting yourself up for failure.

☐ **Emotions are not enough**
Emotions are not executable and can lead you down the wrong path.

☐ **Financial Alignment**
Financial alignment connects your goals and actions to your internal value system.

☐ **Internal Value System**
When your values are properly transferred into financial goals you will feel a sense of satisfaction from taking the action necessary to reach those goals.

☐ **S.M.A.R.T Goals**
Goals that are specific, measurable, attainable, relevant, and time-bound.

☐ **Use a Calendar**

Use your calendar to set aside time for you and your family to do weekly and monthly financial check-ins

☐ **What works for you?**
Money Management is not one size fits all strategy. Find what works for you.

# QUIZ

1.  Who should have a financial strategy?
    (A) Only people who are bad with money.
    (B) People who are looking to build wealth
    (C) A strategy is not really necessary

2.  I recommend that you plan your budget:
    (A) Monthly
    (B) Weekly
    (C) Daily

3.  I recommend that you track your budget:
    (A) Monthly
    (B) Weekly
    (C) Daily

4.  The S in S.M.A.R.T stands for strategic:
    (A) True
    (B) False

    If   false,   what   does   it   stand   for?

    _____

5.  You need to spend at least 40 hours/wk focusing
    on your money in order to build wealth.
    (A) True
    (B) False

# DELIVERABLE

## Creating Financial Alignment

1. What are your top 3 values?
   - ○ _Comfort_
   - ○ _friends & family_
   - ○ _time off to enjoy new places_

2. What are your S.M.A.R.T goals? What would you like to happen in your life in the next 5-10 years?

2022 (27)
-
2027 (32)

   - ○ _purchase my first property_
   - ○ _pay off student loans/car note_
   - ○ _live INDEPENDENTLY_
   - ○ _take a vacation/trip abroad_
   - ○ _save $10K across all my accounts (2K/5K/3K)_
   - ○ _____

3. Of these goals, which are priorities right now?
   - ○ _pay off student loans_
   - ○ _live INDEPENDENTLY_

4. In order to reach your prioritized goals, what actions are you taking?
   - ○ _saving $250/month in personal savings/IRA_
   - ○ _automate all payments_
   - ○ _writing things down in financial notebook_

5. How will you feel when reach your goals?
   _Satisfied. Elated. Successful. Proud._

"Don't tell me where your priorities are. Show me where you spend your money and I'll tell you what they are."

-James W. Frick

# Chapter 3:

# BUILDING A BUDGET

After creating an overarching financial strategy get to work developing the specific components, starting with a budget. Your budget is the embodiment of your internal value system and details how you will use your financial resources. It demonstrates exactly how you plan to take action toward your financial goals. While your financial strategy outlines what you will do, your budget is a major element of how you will do it. Don't rush it. Give your budget the time and attention that it deserves since it is the backbone that will help drive your financial decision-making.

Not having a budget is huge handicap if building wealth is your objective, especially during an economic recession. According to a report from CNN.com, 76% of Americans are currently living paycheck to paycheck. Yet, most do not use this basic tool that could help maximize resources. Don't get me wrong. I understand that there are pervasive social justice issues that give rise to economic hardship. However, there are many ways that we can control our financial destiny and that is where we have to start. Creating a budget forces you to face your financial situation head-on. Let's be honest, our relationship with money can be an emotional rollercoaster of fun, guilt, and everything in between. Like a relationship, money can cause feelings of stress, guilt, fear, and insecurity. And just like one might avoid an ex-boyfriend or girlfriend, we often avoid dealing with our money issues. It's textbook avoidance and I have done it many times.

When faced with the prospect of reviewing your financial baggage it might seem easier to ignore it and hope for the best. This is why so many people avoid opening bills or don't know the total amount of their student loan debt. This doesn't help and only exacerbates the problem. Unlike your ex, your relationship with money isn't going anywhere. It is not in your best interest to ignore it or neglect it. Instead, you should confront your financial demons so that your financial situation can begin to flourish.

Creating a comprehensive budget might not rank very high on your list of fun things to do (although I really enjoy it), but it should definitely be considered a necessity. Maintaining a position of dislike or indifference is futile. Instead, I suggest you change your attitude and fall in love with what budgeting can do for you. Less than 25% of Americans have a 6-month emergency fund and 27% have absolutely no savings at all. Um, that's crazy. Having a budget can help you build up your emergency fund, plan for the future, and save for retirement, which is obviously a lot more than everyone else is doing.

Once you accept that a budget is a necessary tool, you can begin to plan for the unexpected and the inevitable. In life, there are a number of events that are outside of our control and that we cannot plan for. Perhaps your car breaks down and you need a new one or your hot water tank stops working and you need to call a repairman. This is where your emergency fund comes in. But what about the important life events that you can plan for? Even though our lives are not completely planned out, there is certainly a basic blueprint. For the most part, you are going to graduate from college, get a job, move into an apartment, buy a car, get married, buy a house, have kids, send them to college, and then retire. Everyone's life will be different, but it will include at least some of these components. My question to you is that if you know you are likely to encounter these events, how are you planning for them?

In the book *The Millionaire Next Door*, authors Danko and Stanley explain that most millionaires keep a budget and are very knowledgeable about the particulars of their finances. I would venture to say that this attention to detail (which can come from spending as little as one hour per month on your finances) is critical to maintaining wealth over long periods of time. Think about it. Just because someone has money does not mean that they are wealthy or that they will be able to maintain wealth. Time and time again we see athletes fall from billions to bankruptcy and lottery winners go from rags to riches to rags again. I believe that the message is clear. Wealth disparities are not just about money. It is also about knowledge and decisions.

From the United States government to the everyday citizen it is clear that we are missing something when it comes to basic financial principles. And budgeting is perhaps among the most fundamental of those principles. Do you know how much money you have coming in and going out every month? Are you aware of how much you spend dining out, buying clothes or hanging out with friends? Budgeting can help you get a handle on your financial situation. Knowledge of your financial situation is perhaps the most powerful in driving healthy decisions. From understanding where you are now, you can begin to plan for the future. Below is an explanation of basic budgeting concepts.

## Know Where Your Money Goes

When planning out your budget, every single dollar counts and should be working on your behalf to make your financial dreams a reality. Thus, being watchful about how much money is coming and going out is important. I'm a money nerd so I enjoy keeping an eye on my financial progress and it has certainly paid off. Recently, as I was going through my normal financial routine I noticed that something was not right. Every morning I click on my bank app to check out my available balance, just to keep it top of mind. I usually just glance at it and go about my day but this time I noticed that quite a lot of money was missing. I keep all bills scheduled on my calendar so I took a look to see if I had any bills scheduled for that day. I had none.

After researching the issue further I realized that a company had wrongfully charged me for services that I did not receive. To make things worse, this was the second time that they had billed me. In the previous month I had not yet started my daily money management regiment and sure enough, it had almost cost me over $150. It took a few days to straighten out the issue but I eventually did get the charges reversed. This is just one example of why you should pay attention to where your money is going.

To have a better understanding of where your money is going, first identify how much money you have coming in and on what days. Knowing what days your bills are due is important so don't neglect to record that information. Use your calendar as a planning tool to help keep these dates top of mind so that nothing falls through the cracks. Remember to use your net monthly income. You need to understand how much money you have that is actually available for spending. If you don't have a steady monthly income, try your best to use a good average.

Next, try to get a realistic picture of how much is going out every month. This should be broken down into spending, saving, and investing. Each of these categories is a beast of it's own so we shall tackle them separately.

*Spending*

Spending needs no introduction. Most of us are very familiar with this portion of the budget because it seems to come so naturally. Going forward, all spending should pass through the filter of your goals and priorities. Before money leaves your hand evaluate whether or not you are spending in a manner that will help you reach your goals. When creating your spending plan identify all of the things that you spend money on from every day items to bill payments. To keep you honest reference the last 3 months of your bank statements. That should give you a good idea of how much you are spending on different items. It will also help you identify things you might otherwise forget like books, entertainment, or that last minute trip to Target. If you know that you are prone to shopping sprees and impulse purchases, don't put yourself in those situations. When it comes to spending preventative measures work best as you work to build up the will power to say "no" even when you want to say "yes".

*Savings*

The savings portion is the most fun, useful, and underutilized part of the budget. It is my favorite budgeting component because it goes beyond the bills and daily spending that I am faced with today, and allows me to create the future that I want. If I want to go to Europe, I save for it. If I want to take a trip to visit family for the holidays, I save for it. Any time that I want to make something happen in the future, I figure out what I need to do make it happen. And whenever I go on a big trip, take an international vacation or treat myself to a spa day while still having money in the bank, I know that the system is working.

After college I really wanted to take a Mediterranean cruise with my friends once. And guess what, I actually did. I saved for a year and a half and people thought that I was crazy. I was talking to people about a vacation that was more than a year away. People asked me, "Is it really necessary to plan that far out?" Well, maybe not. But by planning so far out the trip was not a financial burden, I had something to look forward to and a reason to happily be frugal. Eventually I was able to travel internationally for the fist time. And guess what. Many of the people who thought I was crazy had never traveled internationally. You'll never guess why…because they did not have enough money! I rest my case.

Setting up a savings plan is simple. You see, banks actually have these things called "savings accounts" that you can use to safely store your money. I'm kidding. In the wake of failing banks and questionable financial practices, our generation is not the most trusting when it comes to big financial institutions. In fact, there is actually a thing called "The Unbank" that helps to facilitate financial transactions for people who do not have bank accounts. Well, despite bank challenges, I would still encourage you to have a bank account. You just have to be smart about it. Make sure that your bank is FDIC ensured and that it offers no or low monthly fees. Also, be open to exploring credit unions for your banking options since credit unions are more likely to cater to the needs of their customers instead of primarily trying to make money.

A savings account can be a good place to store a portion of your savings but I caution you against using one catchall account for all of your savings. I mentioned that all of your money should have a purpose and saving for savings sake does not meet the criteria. You might be one of the few people that are able to succeed with such a strategy, but when your savings account does not have a designated purpose attached to it like wedding, car, or house, it can be easy to repurpose those funds for whatever you need at the moment, which kind of defeats the whole purpose. By giving your money a specific purpose, you can be much more intentional about getting the things you want out of life. Plus, early planning will prevent future stress and worry while helping you build real long-term wealth.

*Investing*

Don't skip this section. I know that so many people think that investing is hard and intimidating, but if you read my story in the beginning then you know that it is not. I started investing with no money and no clue. But over time, I gained both. If you can overcome your fear and get started, it will help you to get on the right path. I am not an investment advisor and do not want to pretend like I can give you advice about how to pick stocks, but apparently, neither can anyone on wall street. Even the professionals rarely consistently beat the market. In Peter Allen's book, he talks about how a group of third graders developed a simulated stock portfolio of their own that blew away most fund managers. These third graders understood a simplistic principle: Invest in what you know.

The point though is that even if you don't know what to do, Google it. Our twenties are the time to take risks. Even if something goes wrong, it won't kill you. You'll be fine. Give it a try. I would not be where I am today had it not been for the fact that I started investing as a sophomore in college. I am grateful everyday that I was bold enough to take the plunge. Financial Freedom is for those who are willing to take risks. For those who want the illusion of security, you can remain in the 9-5 rat race and retire just barely able to sustain yourself. 73% of Americans say that they wish they had saved more for retirement. If you don't want to be like them, this is your opportunity to make a change that will certainly change your life. And you can always work with a financial advisor to get started. Just know that over the long haul, you will be paying them a hefty sum. But, earning something and having a peace of mind is certainly better than not doing anything at all. I can't go into detail because I don't want the SEC to come pick me up and take me away, but if you go to a site like troweprice.com or fidelity.com you will find that investing is not as hard as it might seem. You just have to start somewhere.

## Budgeting Allocation Percentages

When planning your budget, it can be hard to know if you are spending too much in any one category. Here are some guidelines to help give you an idea. They are specifically tailored for young adults, not the adult population at large.

22% Housing

15% Utilities

12% Food

10% Transportation

10% Debt Repayment

10% Savings

6% Investing

5% Clothing

5% Entertainment

5% Car Insurance

**<u>Practical Strategies</u>**

So far, we have covered the technical aspects of budgeting. And while the knowledge is great, it will be useless if you can't conceptualize how to put this stuff into action. My clients struggle with this all of the time. Because even when you know what to do, it can be hard to follow through. So, to help you figure out the best to way manage your finances, take a look at these examples from some anonymous young adults.

*Keep it Separate:*

When I am managing my finances every month, I like to keep everything separate and automatic. I have one bank account for my bills and another for everything else. When I receive my check, it is automatically split between both of these accounts. Once my paycheck is allocated, my bills are paid automatically. Also, every month a certain amount of money is transferred directly to my savings and investing accounts. So, whatever is in my bank account is money that I can spend freely. Once it is gone it's gone.

*Save Like Crazy*

I don't like to focus on the little details of money management but I do want to build wealth and become a millionaire. So, I try to live on as little as possible and save everything else. I am also investing. I know that I have some things to work on but I feel great knowing that I am consistently saving as much as I can every month. The next step is to figure out what I want to do with it and then determine where I should put it to get the highest ROI.

*Stay Vigilant*

At the beginning of the month I sit down and take a look at my finances at a high level. I look at how my net worth has changed over time and how much work I need to do to reach my long-term goals. In order to make sure that I actually do this I set up a calendar appointment for the first day of every month. I also have appointments set up for every Sunday so that I can plan out my week.

Remember that there are many ways to manage your finances and that what gets measured gets results. So, start with something but then move towards a system that will allow you to keep track of your growth.

# RECAP

This chapter focuses on creating a budget that will help you get on the fast track to wealth creation.

☐ **Budget**
Your goals and priorities should be represented in your budget. Be sure to spend in a way that is in line with what you really want.

☐ **Act with Clarity**
Having a budget gives you clear insight into your financial habits and allows you to face them and fix them head on.

☐ **Save more spend less**
The most basic concept of budgeting is to ensure that your income is larger than your expenses. Otherwise, you will quickly go into debt. Many ignore this.

☐ **Plan for the unexpected**
Build your emergency fund so that you do not have to use your savings or investments to cover unexpected expenses.

☐ **Plan for Expected Events**
Save up for important life events so that you do not have to dip into your investments to cover them.

☐ **What works for you?**
There are many different budgeting styles. Find one that will work for you.

# QUIZ

1. What % of Americans lives check to check?
   (A) Less than 20%
   (B) About 50%
   (C) More than 70%

2. What are the 3 components of a budget?
   (A) Spending, Saving, Investing
   (B) Spending, Saving, Net worth
   (C) Assets, Liabilities, Net worth

3. According to our guide, what % of income should go toward housing?
   (A) 15%
   (B) 22%
   (C) 30%

4. You should wait to start investing until you acquire more assets:
   (A) True
   (B) False

# DELIVERABLE

*monthly*

Complete Your Budget:
Download our budget form from the Facebook page.
Here are some important questions that you should answer:

1. What is your total income? $ ~~$~~ 1521.72

2. What are your total expenses? $ 1100.46
   (inc. $280 → ½ savings, ½ JRA)

3. Are your expenses less than your income? (Y) or
   N)

4. Is there anything in your budget that you would like
   to (or need to) adjust?
   Metrofare; increasing how much I spend

5. What are your top 4 expenses? Does it align with
   your goals and priorities?
   - Car note ($438.46)
   - Student loans ($122)
   - Savings ($280)

6. How much are you saving? $ 280 % ~18

7. How much are you investing? $ 0 % 0

8. What do you need to change?
   My investing habits

80

"If you think nobody cares if you're alive, try missing a couple of car payments."

- Earl Wilson

# Chapter 4:

# DEMOLISHING DEBT

To be in debt simply means that you owe something to someone. It means that in some way, shape, or form you took more than you could afford and will eventually have to pay it back...with interest. To put it eloquently, DEBT SUCKS. And yet, it is irresistible at the same time. Our relationship with debt is much like fraternizing with the enemy. Every once in a while we get something out of it but we know from the beginning that it probably won't end well.

Psychologically, our minds are not wired to fully comprehend the consequences of taking out a loan. We have this thing about instant gratification. Instead of deeply considering the long-term consequences of our actions, we are somewhat blinded by our present desires. Additionally, we are overly optimistic about what the future will bring. Instead of weighing all options (like the possibility of losing a job) we tend to believe that our situation will stay the same or get better, which means that we will be able to pay off our loans right? Well, the answer is maybe and eventually.

When you take out a loan, typically you get a lump sum of money that must be paid back over a period time with a fixed or variable interest rate. This means that you are actually going to have to pay extra for the privilege of using someone else's money, which is fair enough. The funny thing is that we loan money to banks all the time. You know that money in your checking or saving accounts? Banks use that to invest and make money all while paying you a miserable interest rate. But when the tables are turned, they intend to make a profit. And who can really blame them as long as they do it ethically. It is their job to make money and it your job to protect yours. In an ideal situation all parties profit from the transaction. You get what you want and the banks collect interest. But since when has anything ever operated ideally? Usually someone is going to win and someone is going to lose.

According to the Federal Reserve Bank of New York, total household debt in the United States is just over $11 Trillion. According to a deconstruction of the numbers from the Washington Post, 71% is from mortgages, 9% from student loan debt, and 13% from auto and credit card debt. To provide context for how we are managing this, the Daily Finance says "more than $1 trillion of our current debt load is delinquent, and nearly $800 billion has been delinquent for more than 90 days." Additionally, those that are not delinquent are likely going to find it difficult to retire. The article goes on to say "the study shows that we're burning through our savings to pay our debts down. The overall net worth of the average American is down nearly 40% from 2007 to 2010." The debt dilemma is not something that you want to get tangled up in.

Despite these numbers, we continue to rely on debt to help us obtain the accessories that are so deeply embedded within our value system. In many ways, we have become dependent on debt. It allows us to live beyond our current resources so that we can have the things that we could not otherwise afford. Some of these things are superfluous like dresses and shoes, but others seem essential. In our minds, it is absolutely critical that we have a college education, a car, and a home. And without debt, it would be impossible for many people to achieve them.

Like most things, debt is not inherently bad. It is simply another financial instrument that can be wielded for good or evil. If you approach debt with the right knowledge, perspective, and insight, it is much more likely that the transaction will work out favorably. Unfortunately, because we lack a comprehensive personal finance education, we do not always have the tools that will help us make good decisions. So, I am not opposed to all debt but in its current form it seems to be far too commonplace. It has become the rule instead of the exception. While debt can absolutely be leveraged to build wealth, you have to be smart about it. Taking on too much debt is largely what prompted our current economic recession. It would be smart to use it cautiously and wisely despite the fact that it has pervasively permeated all levels of society.

## Types of Debt

### Student Loan Debt

Student loan debt in particular is the arch nemesis of 20-somethings all across America. Education costs continue to rise, and guess what...so does the unemployment rate. Something just doesn't feel right about paying for an education that doesn't really do what you thought it would. For many of my clients it is down right depressing. That might be the case for you too.

While young adults struggle to pay off student loans our lawmakers stand idly by watching the situation get even worse. In July of 2013, the Huffington Post writes that interest rates for subsidized Stafford loans doubled from 3.4% to 6.8% after "congressional inaction". Wait. WHAT? Believe it or not, student loan interest rates doubled and in many cases, students did not even notice. But I bet they will when they have to pay it back. Lawmakers were aware of the upcoming deadline but were unable to reach a "deal".

At this moment, I realized that there was no one in Washington fighting for my interests or yours. Student loans are big business and lets face it, banks are doing whatever they can to make an extra buck. I only emphasize this to say that if you think someone else is going to fight your battles for you, you are very much mistaken. The fact of the matter is that if you want a safety net, you are going to have to nit it yourself. This is just one of many examples showcasing congressional ineffectiveness. Considering the fiscal cliff and the government shut down, I do not feel that young adults have been personally singled out. However, I am telling you that if you do not wake up, pay attention, and start planning for your future, you are going to be in trouble.

I place a huge emphasis on student loan debt because it could easily become the mortgage crisis of our generation. In many instances we are "degree poor" meaning that we paid too much money for a piece of paper that has not delivered the value that we had hoped. And unfortunately, student loan debt is not our only challenge. In fact, it magnifies other financial challenges creating a snowball effect that has had dire consequences for the financial prospects of young adults. For example, you start your life in the real world $25K in debt. Do you really want to buy a car? If you do, your debt ticket just went up. What about getting married, buying a home, or starting a family? How on earth can someone get out of debt when life continues to happen so quickly?

The best safeguard against making poor financial decisions is to be educated. Here are some terms you should know regarding student loan debt.

Interest:

Interest is the amount that banks charge you to use their money over a certain period of time. When a bank gives you a loan, they charge you interest so that they can make money. This means that you will have to pay back the principle (what you borrowed) in addition to interest (how much the bank is charging you expressed as a percentage). Since banks typically charge interest monthly, we use the compound interest formula:

$$\text{Compound Interest} = P[(1+i)^n - 1]$$

If you were to take out a subsidized Stafford loan of $1000 at an interest rate of 3.4% for 3 years your interest would be $53.28. However, if interest rates double, your total finance charge would be $108.29. Before taking on a loan, be sure to shop around for the best rates. Look at the interest rate, the time period, and most of all, the total interest paid. The more money you take out, the more interest you will end up paying.

ROI:

This is a financial acronym that stands for return on investment. Investopedia.com describes it as "a performance measure used to evaluate the efficiency of an investment or to compare the efficiency of a number of different investments." In layman's terms, it is a measure of how much bang you get for your buck. ROI is expressed as a percentage or a ratio. It is calculated accordingly:

$$\frac{(\text{Gain From Investment- Cost of Investment})}{\text{Cost of Investment}}$$

A higher percentage means a better return, and a better return means a better investment. In this equation there are only two variables to consider, including how much you will gain from an investment and how much it will cost. When determining what you will gain you should consider the tangibles as well as the intangibles. Tangible benefits might include competitiveness or earning potential. Intangible benefits could be status or expanding your worldview.

Ultimately, you want to avoid being what I like to call "degree poor" meaning that your education does not afford the economic benefits that you hoped it would.

After evaluating the costs and benefits of multiple scenarios, ultimately choose what works best for you. In my experience, intangible benefits are more emotion driven and can sometimes blind you to what will really make a difference in the end.

*Mortgage Debt:*

Mortgages make up the vast majority of all household debt. A home is a symbol of family and status and helps us feel like we have finally settled down into adulthood. In many ways, it is the very embodiment of the American dream. But, in recent years mortgages have caused the nightmare that is our current economic recession. To simplify, too many people purchased homes they could not afford and ended up defaulting. This caused a ripple effect that we are still feeling today.

When considering the purchase of a new home, it is easy to rely heavily on emotion, especially given our symbolic view of what a home represents. However, in order to make a good decision about a home purchase you must minimize (not necessarily eliminate) your emotional attachment and view it as an investment. Relying more heavily on numbers will help to ensure that this is a decision you can stand behind now and in the future.

As an investment, you will want to consider your reason for buying, your current priorities, how long you plan to hold it, and what return you will get over time.

Keep in mind that taking on a mortgage is a huge responsibility and is not something that you can readily get out of. That being said, owning a home can be a great investment decision if you understand the different variables you need to take into consideration.

Down payment:

A down payment is how much money you put down towards the purchase of your home. The standard is 20% of the total cost of the home. If you have less than 20% you will have to pay additional monthly insurance in the form of PMI (see below). Sometimes, down payment assistance is available from different sources.

Example:

If you would like to purchase a home that cost's $100,000 you will need to put down 20% or $20,000. You will use a bank to finance the other 80% or $80,000. Of course, the bank will charge you for borrowing $80,000 in the form of monthly mortgage payments. (see below)

Homeowner's Insurance:

A type of property insurance that protects the value of your home if something should happen to it. The bank will require that you have insurance in order to protect their investment.

Cost of Improvements:

Be sure to calculate the cost of all repairs and improvements that you plan to do on the home and add this to the total cost of the home when doing any ROI or cost benefit analysis. It is easy to overlook this but little projects add up and can turn a good investment into a bad investment. Also, if you put money into your home through improvements, you will want to consider whether or not it will increase the property value sufficiently for you to make your investment back in the event that you sell.

Interest: See interest explanation above.

Mortgage Payments:

Your monthly mortgage payment will consider be based on the amount of the loan, interest rate, and length of time. There are other components like points and lenders fees that you will want to discuss with your realtor.

PMI: Private Mortgage Insurance

If you do not have 20%of the total loan amount available for a down payment, banks will charge you additional interest to make up for it. Essentially, the 20% is meant to protect their investment and if you do not have it then they must get assurance somewhere else. In this case, in the form of PMI

*Car Loan:*

Financing your car might seem like a good idea at the time but it rarely is. Cars depreciate in value the minute you drive them off the lot. This makes them a very poor investment. Your car is a liability and with gas prices soaring upward, it is sure to take a lot of money out of your pocket. And let's not forget about insurance. When you want a car, the best way to go about getting one is to save up for it and skip the monthly payments and debt load. To make this as plain as possible, it is almost never a good idea to finance a car. Instead, do the hard work and save up for the car you want. You will be happy that you did.

*Credit Cards:*

Credit cards have caused many an impoverished person. It is so easy to get caught up in the idea of buying now and paying later, but it very easy for your debt to spiral out of control. When you use your credit card, this is not free money. You must pay for the use of that money for as long as you carry a balance. In the end, it's usually not worth it. Don't use credit to buy things you could not otherwise afford.

## The Effects of Debt

Debt does not just affect your finances. We all know how important money is to our day-to-day lives and how it can permeate all other thoughts. When you think about it, it is quite astonishing how our lives consist of so many financial transactions. It does not matter if you are buying groceries or paying the mortgage, you will find it difficult to get through a day without making a single purchase. Thoughts of money are often amplified when debt is involved. Debt impacts you emotionally and physically

Debt can be a mental burden that makes it difficult for you to enjoy other areas of your life. People typically deal with debt in three ways. There are some people who have a good handle on their debt. They understand their total debt picture and feel comfortable meeting the monthly payments. Unfortunately most people do not fall into this category. The majority of young adults end up having a dysfunctional attitude toward debt, which does not bode well for their financial future.

On one half of the coin you have those that are overcome with fear and shame. Every time they spend a dime on anything that is even remotely enjoyable and not absolutely necessary there is an immediate feeling of guilt because that money could have gone toward paying down other financial obligations. The guilt does not improve financial behavior and instead causes them to turn a blind eye to their poor decision-making. You can see how this creates a spiraling cycle that only leads to more bad decisions and thus more debt.

On the other hand, you have those that feel no guilt and are likely in a state of denial. Instead of facing the problem head on, they act as if there is no problem and simply go on with life as usual numb to the financial burden that is soon to come crushing down. People who are in denial refuse to get a handle on their total debt picture and think that if they just ignore it then it's not really there.

Managing debt does not have to be such an exhausting burden. It's obviously not fun, but when you put it within the context of a larger financial plan, hopefully you can begin to see the light at the end of the tunnel. Tackling your debt with clarity and purpose will give you peace of mind you need to build a stable financial foundation. As I mentioned, in 2011, total student loan debt passed the trillion-dollar level for the first time ever in history. I would feel quite justified in stating this same statistic 5 more times because it needs to sink in. To be honest, my brain can barely conceptualize $1 trillion. When you consider that this number does not include consumer debt or mortgages, it is easy to draw the conclusion that young adults are currently experiencing serious financial stress. Our parents may have started with nothing, but on average we are starting our adult lives more than $25,000 in the hole and it is impacting every area of our adult life.

Student loan debt is not the only hardship of young adults. We graduated or were recently employed during one of the worst economic recessions in history. Because of this, adults 18-34 are experiencing higher than average unemployment rates, which will surely impact earning potential over time. According to Brookings, "young people... will earn approximately 17.5 percent less per year than comparable peers graduating in better labor markets. This lower wage effect is highly persistent, fading away only after 17 years of work." A lower wage means that you will be paying off less debt, saving less money, and investing less in your future. Over time, this will have a drastic impact on your wealth accumulation and your ability to pay off debt unless you take the right precautions.

In order to diminish the impact of debt coupled with a troubled economy, young adults must work twice as hard. Debt is as much apart of the American dream as home ownership and white picket fences. It's the elephant in the room that we never talk about. After all, someone has to finance this big dream of ours because it comes with a hefty price tag. Eliminating your debt is an important step in getting on track to achieving the financial lifestyle that you want for yourself. The best thing that you can do for yourself is to be an educated debt consumer and to use it as little as possible.

Before you take on additional debt, ask yourself these 5 questions:

1.  Do I need this?

2.  Am I getting the best value?

3.  How long will it take me to pay off this debt?

4. What could go wrong? What could happen to prevent me from paying back this loan?

5. If I am unable to pay back this loan due to unforeseen circumstances, what is at risk?

With an investor's eye and mindset you will be able to answer these questions and make a decision that will be best for you. Lastly, just in case you are already in debt, I want to leave you with a debt demolition plan. After all, that is the name of the chapter. You will find it as the deliverable at the end.

# RECAP

This chapter focuses on understanding and managing debt.

☐ **How to get INTO Debt**
By spending more than you actually have. It works every time.

☐ **Student Loan Debt**
Approach student loans cautiously. Student loans could cause the mortgage crisis of our generation.

☐ **Return on Investment**
This is basically a measure of how much bang you get for your buck. Consider this before you make any investment.

☐ **Debt can be a burden**
Debt can be a mental burden that makes it difficult for you to enjoy other areas of your life

☐ **Mortgage Debt**
Makes up the majority of all debt

☐ **Loans**
Before you take out a loan get quotes from different banks. Shop around!

# QUIZ

1. ROI involves two variables including:
   (A) Total Debt and Cost of Loan
   (B) Total Debt and Cost of investment
   (C) Gain from Investment and Cost of Investment

2. What makes up the largest percentage of total debt?
   (A) Student loan debt
   (B) Mortgage Debt
   (C) Credit card debt

3. Your down payment on a home is usually:
   (A) 10%
   (B) 20%
   (C) 30%

4. What makes up the 2nd largest percentage of household debt?

   (A) Credit Card Debt
   (B) Mortgage Debt
   (C) Student Loan Debt

# DELIVERABLE

## Debt Demolition Plan

Loans:

1: Amount: $_____ Interest: ____% MP: $_____
2: Amount: $_____ Interest: ____% MP: $_____
3: Amount: $_____ Interest: ____% MP: $_____
4: Amount: $_____ Interest: ____% MP: $_____
5: Amount: $_____ Interest: ____% MP: $_____

MP= Minimum Payment

Total Loans: $_____
Monthly MP: $_____

Credit Cards:

1: Amount: $_____ Interest: ____% MP: $_____
2: Amount: $_____ Interest: ____% MP: $_____
3: Amount: $_____ Interest: ____% MP: $_____
4: Amount: $_____ Interest: ____% MP: $_____
5: Amount: $_____ Interest: ____% MP: $_____

Total CC Debt: $_____
Monthly MP: $_____

Steps to eliminate debt:

1. Identify the credit card or loan that has the lowest balance.
2. Use a debt demolition payment to pay down this debt as quickly as possible.
3. Continue paying the minimum payment on all other forms of debt.
4. Once you pay off one credit card or loan, continue to the next. Use your entire debt demolition payment to speed up payment.
5. Once you have gained momentum, you can get even savvier. Pay of the loan or credit card that will cost you the most over time.

"Frugality includes all the other virtues."

-Cicero

# Chapter 5:

# CORRECTING YOUR CREDIT

After such an exhilarating conversation about debt, it is only natural that we transition into our discussion on credit. Essentially, they are two sides of the same coin. Credit gives you the ability to get something now and pay for it later opening the door to debt. Our relationship with credit is what gives rise to a credit score, which is a financial report card that expresses our credit worthiness to others. In this chapter we will discuss the responsible use of credit and the factors that impact your credit score.

Until you enter the real world, it is a little known fact how important it is to establish a healthy credit history. This certainly varies person to person, but in my experience college students are largely unaware of how credit cards will impact them in the future. Financial institutions take advantage of this to prey on college students in the hopes that they will run up their credit before they even leave college. Unfortunately, many do.

Upon graduating college, the average student is about $5,000 in credit card debt. When added to the $25,000 of student loan debt, this is certainly not a pretty picture. Students use credit cards for anything from food to college tuition, and everything in between. Sometimes we rely on credit instead of exhausting all of our resources to manage expenses up front. Since we are able to get what we now and pay for it later, we often opt to pay for it later even though later will come sooner than we think. Again, it's that issue of instant gratification over long-term consequences.

Using credit is not bad and is actually necessary. It wasn't until my senior year of college that I learned the importance of establishing a good credit history early. But, in order to build a good credit history you must engage in healthy credit behavior. Here are 7 Habits of Healthy Credit Behavior:

- Pick a credit card that has the best interest rate
- Choose a card that has no annual fees
- Don't spend more than you can afford
- Don't make it a habit to carry large balances
- Track your spending
- Make more than the minimum payments

- Remember that it is ~~easier to get into debt than it is to get out of it.~~

By following these tips on how to wisely use your credit, you can begin to establish a credit history that will serve you well through out your life. It is common for your credit history to be considered when getting an apartment, buying a home, getting a job, or even when applying for some utilities. By focusing on your credit score early, you will save yourself a lot of trouble.

A Credit Score is a number that tells the rest of the world if they should trust you with money. There are three major credit bureaus including TransUnion, Experian, and Equifax. The credit scores from each bureau should be similar, but they are never the same because each bureau considers slightly different factors. Credit scores are useful because they are a way for different institutions to assess your "financial character". If a friend of yours asked to borrow money, you would use your knowledge of their moral disposition to inform your decision-making. But what if the person who wanted to get something on credit was not your friend? How would you decide whether or not to lend them money?

In olden days when our financial infrastructure was not as developed, there was no such thing as a credit score. The only way to determine whether or not someone would pay you back was by judging his or her character. In this time integrity and character was very important because it was used to facilitate financial interactions. In fact, the phrase, "my word is my bond" can be understood to mean that my word is as good as money. It was an assurance that someone could be trusted to pay his or her debt. But today we do not have to rely on a person's word. Companies use credit histories to get a play by play of our financial lifestyles.

A bad credit score might initially seem like nothing more than an annoyance, but it can actually cost you money. When your credit score is low, it is an indication that if you take out a loan, you just might not pay it back. This makes you a risk to lenders. To provide a real life example, what if you knew that your friend Kiana borrowed money from Lindsey but never paid her back. Would you feel confident loaning money to Kiana in the future? Perhaps you would be kind enough to give her another chance, but you would probably be more cautious this time around. And that is exactly how financial institutions respond. Who knew they could be so human!

If you have a low credit score, banks are going to see you as a risk. This means that they are going to charge you a higher interest rate to compensate for the risk, and if you are buying a home, they might require a larger down payment. A higher interest rate means that your cost of borrowing money has increased, and a higher down payment could mean less liquidity and leverage for you. If your credit score is too bad, it is unlikely that financial institutions will want to deal with you at all.

Credit Ratings:

750-850: Excellent

700-749: Very Good

650-699: Good

600-649: Average

550-599: Poor

549 and below: Very Poor

These credit ratings are one way that financial institutions assess your credit worthiness. There are five important factors that impact this score:

Payment history (30%):

Your payment history has the greatest impact on your credit score. It tells lenders how reliable you are paying your bills on time. If you are late paying a bill, it is not reported to the credit union unless you have been late for over one month. Your credit history actually shows how late you were month by month. A payment that is late for more than 30 days is considered delinquent. If you were late for 90 days or more, this becomes a huge red flag on your credit score.

Amount of debt (30%):

Banks like you to have some debt, but not too much. They especially want to make sure that you are not using up all of your available credit. For example, if you have a total credit limit of $1000, you should not use more than $300 of it. If you use more, it will begin to hurt your credit score. You should only be using 30% of the total credit you have available to you!

### Length of history (15%):

A more established credit history helps lenders feel comfortable that they have a well-rounded view of your financial behaviors. With a short credit history, banks are not as trusting because they do not yet know what you are capable of. This is why it is so important to start establishing your credit history while you are still in college, as long as you do it the right way.

### New credit (10%):

Banks don't like to see you applying for multiple credit cards. Every time you send in a credit application, it costs you a few points off of your credit score. However, if you are shopping around for a car loan or something like that, you will only be dinged once.

### Types of credit (10%):

Try to have a balanced debt portfolio. This might include student loan debt, credit cards, and a mortgage. Having a mix of credit products make banks happy. I'm not really sure why.

Equipped with this information, you are completely empowered to improve your credit score. And believe it or not, it does not take a long time. Credit repair companies take advantage of people who are looking for a quick fix, but there are no quick fixes where your credit score is concerned. The best thing that you can do is put in the work and watch your credit score improve slowly but surely. If you choose not to put in the work to develop a good credit score, it will affect you in many ways during your lifetime:

Getting an apartment:

Once you leave college and are looking for an apartment to start your new life, there is a good chance that your landlord will want to see your credit score. If you have abused your credit during your college years this could have several negative consequences. You might be required to leave a larger security deposit, your month-to-month rent might be raised, or you might be disqualified altogether. No landlord wants to deal with a tenant that might not pay his or her rent.

Getting a job:

Nowadays, many employers look at your credit score as a measure of responsibility and integrity. If you have bad credit, this might be a sign to an employer that they do not want to bring you on as an asset to the team. Your credit score could actually cause you to lose out on a job opportunity.

Buying a house:

When buying a home, your credit score is very important. Your credit score is directly related to your interest rate, and since this interest rate will be paid over the course of 15 or 30 years, even a small percentage increase will have a drastic impact on your overall payment. Banks also might require you to make a larger down payment.

Purchasing a car:

Similar to purchasing a house, the better your credit score, the better interest rate you are likely to receive from your lender.

Hopefully, this chapter has impressed upon you how much your credit can impact other areas of your life. The sooner you understand how credit works, the sooner you can start making decisions that will positively affect you. Having a good credit score is largely about knowing how to play the game. Now, you do!

# RECAP

This chapter focuses on understanding how use credit responsibly to avoid debt and a bad credit score.

☐ **Credit**
Allows you to get what you want now while paying for it later. Opens the door to debt if abused.

☐ **Establish Credit History Early**
Establish your credit history early by responsibly using credit cards while in college. Better to have it and not need it than to need it and not be able to get it.

☐ **Healthy Credit Behavior**
Refer back to the "7 Habits of Healthy Credit Behavior" to ensure that you use your credit cards wisely.

☐ **Credit Scores**
Your credit score is essential to getting access to low and affordable interest rates.

☐ **Mortgage Debt**
Mortgage debt makes up the majority of all debt

## ☐ Loans

Before you take out a loan get quotes from different banks. Shop around!

# QUIZ

1. The best time to establish credit history is:
   (A) In college
   (B) After college
   (C) Right before you purchase your first home

2. Credit is there to help you cover day-to-day expenses that you might not otherwise be able to afford.
   (A) True
   (B) False

3. Which of the following is a good example of healthy credit card behavior:
   (A) Keeping a large revolving balance
   (B) Finding a credit card with low interest rates
   (C) Only make the minimum payments on all cards

4. You need to focus on your credit score from all 3 bureaus:
   (A) True
   (B) False

5. An average credit score is considered:
   (A) 750-850
   (B) 700-749
   (C) 600-649

# DELIVERABLE

Technology can be a great to help you manage your finances. By signing up for the below websites, you will gain insights that will allow you to make better financial decisions. Each of the below sites serve a different purpose, from obtaining your credit score to better understanding student loans.

1. Sign up for creditkarma.com
2. Sign up for mint.com
3. Sign up for tuition.io

"If you would be wealthy, think of saving as well as getting."

-Ben Franklin

# Chapter 6:

# INCREASING INCOME

You cannot get rich and build wealth without making money. That much is obvious. That is, unless you plan on winning the lottery or inheriting a small fortune. However, if that is not the case, then making money is at least of some importance, but perhaps not the most important. You see, making money and keeping money are very different things and just because one might make more money, this does not mean that they will make better financial decisions. If you have not fully grasped the financial principals of budgeting, building credit, and demolishing debt, money will easily slip through your fingers. Many pro athletes can attest to this fact.

Monthly income is a measurable number that affects our day-to-day life. It is obvious that a greater income provides more opportunities to build wealth, but maximizing your income can actually provide more opportunities to build wealth as well. Income is often seen as a set number, but I have come to learn that there is room for interpretation. One day, a very long time ago,

I read a statement that completely changed the way that I thought about money. At the time I did not understand it, but the concept was impressed upon me nonetheless. I can't remember exactly what I was reading; I believe it was an article. It stated that whenever you buy something on sale, you are essentially increasing your income. This thought was baffling to me at the time. I could not understand how buying something for less could put more real money in my pocket, but I believe that I understand it more fully now. Let me explain by way of example:

|        | A      | B      |
|--------|--------|--------|
| House: | $700   | $1000  |
| Car:   | $200   | $400   |
| Food:  | $200   | $300   |
| Total: | $1100  | $1700  |

In this example, let's assume that person A and B both have equal income. If this is the case, just based on the facts that we have, person A has $600 more than Person B, even if they have the same income. Person A can use this additional income to build wealth by saving or investing, or they can use it for more immediate pleasures that have no long-term benefits. In this case, they would be no better off than person B in the long run. The point is that just by spending less money, you can have more.

Here's another example…

|        | A        | B        |
|--------|----------|----------|
| Makes  | $45,000  | $50,000  |
| Spends | $35,000  | $52,000  |

In this case, even though person A makes less money, they are in a position to build wealth while person B is positioned to go into debt. This just goes to show that while income is important, it is certainly not the whole story. Even though person B makes les money, they have more opportunity to save and invest.

It is very easy to get consumed with income. But we really need to get consumed with saving, investing, and developing healthy financial habits. It might seem silly for someone to position himself or herself for debt when they could easily be building wealth instead, but it happens very often. Can you imagine what it feels like to go to work everyday and not have anything to show for it outside of what is in your closet? After doing a full budget analysis, many people are left wondering where the heck all of their money has gone. After looking at the monthly numbers, it becomes evident how much money has slipped through the cracks.

According to Investopedia.com, income is defined as "money that an individual receives in exchange for providing a good or service." It is not rocket science but our mindset regarding income is very narrow indeed. We believe that if we do well in grade school, go to college, and get a job, we will be able to make enough money to attain financial freedom. Unfortunately it is not quite this easy. In order to really achieve financial freedom we must learn how to make our money work for us even while we are sleeping.

Contrary to what we have been taught, there is more than one way to make money. In order to attain financial freedom and accelerate your path to wealth, it is essential that you develop multiple income streams across different categories. There are two types of income, active, and passive. Active income is income that you have to work for. This includes working your 9-5 job and even being self-employed if you are your main employee. In this category, you have to work hard for the money. The income that many people overlook, and that the wealthy monopolize, is in the passive income category. Passive income is income made from investments and through business. With passive income, even if you do not show up to a job, you still get paid. In order to crack the code to financial freedom, you have to understand how to start making passive income. These four different categories of income make up what is called the cash flow quadrant and just like anything, you should diversify your holdings.

When I first learned that most millionaires have multiple income streams, I was surprised and baffled. I was surprised because it was such a foreign concept to me and I was baffled because I did not understand why this was not common knowledge. Growing up, I was so focused on having one career and one income stream when I should have been thinking on a much larger scope. As a famous songwriter once said, There's a million ways to get it," so why do we think we should only choose one?

If you knew how to increase your income on your own, I imagine that you would have done it already. In the technological age, opportunity abounds. In the 21st century, many young adults turn to the Internet to make money via blogs, websites, information, and online shops. There is no limit to the things that you can do. If you are creative you can make your own online store on etsy.com to sell unique jewelry or other craft creations. If you like collecting nice things perhaps you use eBay to sell your best vintage finds.

Do you have a unique story or journey that you can share with the world? Of course you do. As you can see with the rise of reality TV, people are obsessed with going deeper into people's lives. You could monetize your journey as a young boy trying to make it to the NBA or mom exploring the high and lows of motherhood. Your ability to create an addition income stream online is only limited by your imagination. You are unique and I believe that you have some gift, talent, or knowledge to share with the world.

There are more ways than ever to monetize your interests and passions. I typically recommend finding income streams that are related to things that you enjoy, while others would recommend putting your efforts behind proven money making strategies. My thoughts are that if you are going to work everyday and put additional energy behind side hustles, they should be something that you enjoy and something that makes money. Keep in mind that I am idealistic and I don't believe you should have to choose between passion and money. I believe that if you do what you love the money will follow. Be creative and I am confident that you will find additional income streams that fit within your lifestyle.

Most young adults rely on a job for their primary income. Moving up the corporate ladder is certainly not my area of expertise but it can't be ignored as a means to increased income. That being said, I recommend that you take advantage of resources such as mentorship and development training within your company to maintain a competitive edge. Also, never be afraid to ask for what you are worth. Any job that you have should value you as an employee and compensate you accordingly. If you are not happy with your job or career, remember that you are in control of your life. Change is not just going to happen, you must initiate it. If you are seeking more advantageous employment, ask yourself what will it take to get you where you want to go. I am not a career coach, but I definitely recommend that you think about how you invest in your education and how that will translate into your career trajectory and your long-term wealth building potential.

# RECAP

This chapter focuses on creating additional income to fuel your path to wealth

- ☐ **Income**
  Income is an important part of building wealth, but it certainly is not the whole story.

- ☐ **Keep your Money**
  Wealth is not about how much money you make, it about how much money you keep.

- ☐ **Maximize Income**
  Making the most of the money that you already have can be incredibly effective on your path to wealth creation.

- ☐ **Multiple Income Streams**
  In order to achieve financial freedom, you need to have several income streams, not just a job.

- ☐ **Cash flow Quadrant**
  Active income is made through working and self-employment. Passive income is made through investments and businesses.

# QUIZ

1.  Income is not the most important factor in
    building wealth:
     (A) True
    (B) False

2.  Which of the following is not apart of the cash
    flow quadrants:
     (A) Income
    (B) Self-Employed
    (C) Employee

3.  It is best to focus on developing one income
    stream:
    (A) True
     (B) False

4.  If you make a large income, it is not necessary to
    closely manage your money:
    (A) True
    (B) False

# DELIVERABLE

## Increase Your Income

1. List 3 ways you can maximize your income to start doing more with what you already have:
   - ○ _SPEND LESS ON FOOD!_
   - ○ _Start investing_
   - ○ _____

2. Identify 3 ways you can use your passion to make money:
   - ○ _Freelance write/blogger_
   - ○ _Copy edit / proofread_
   - ○ _Service via time (?)_
   - ○ _____
   - ○ _____
   - ○ _____

3. Of these options, which will you try first? Outline your ideas:
   _Maybe start freelancing in the new year?_
   _____
   _____
   _____
   _____
   _____
   _____

"Make money your god, and it will plague you like the devil."

- Henry Fielding

# QUIZ ANSWERS

| Chapter 1 | Chapter 2 | Chapter 3 |
|-----------|-----------|-----------|
| 1. C | 1. B | 1. C |
| 2. B | 2. A | 2. A |
| 3. B | 3. B | 3. B |
| 4. B | 4. B | 4. B |
| 5. C | 5. B | |

| Chapter 4 | Chapter 5 | Chapter 6 |
|-----------|-----------|-----------|
| 1. C | 1. A | 1. A |
| 2. B | 2. B | 2. A |
| 3. B | 3. B | 3. B |
| 4. A | 4. A | 4. B |
| | 5. C | |

# STEP-BY-STEP GUIDE

Building wealth is easy. You just have to know what you are doing. It is impossible to go into every single aspect of wealth building within the confines of one book, but we will cover many of the below.

1. Identify goals and priorities
2. Create a budget
3. Improve your credit score
4. Maximize your income
5. Decrease your spending
6. Pay down debt
7. Contribute to your 401k at least to the company match (low cost investments)
8. Open up and max out your IRA (low cost investments)
9. Get Insurance and Plan Estate
10. Buy an investment property instead of a home

# 36 COMMON FINANCIAL MISTAKES

1. Not setting financial goals
2. Not having a budget
3. Going into credit card debt in college
4. Financing a car
5. Not getting a roommate right after college
6. Moving away from home too soon
7. Not having an emergency fund to fall back on
8. Spending more than saving
9. Not developing financial values
10. Living at or beyond your means too early (you should live below your means)
11. Not taking advantage of the tax code
12. Taking on too much student loan debt and becoming degree poor
13. Making late payments and allowing bills to become delinquent
14. Not paying off traffic tickets. These can find their way on your credit history
15. Paying too much money for furniture right out of college. Tastes change
16. Leaving money on the table by not investing in a company sponsored 401K with a match
17. Buying too much furniture out of college. You're probably going to move a lot.

18. Not getting properly insured
19. Paying too much for insurance
20. Not considering the financial implications of children
21. Spending too much money on drinking in clubs. If you must drink, try to do it at home.
22. Eating out too often.
23. Being negatively influenced by broke friends.
24. Valuing things over experiences even though experiences make us happier.
25. Paying full price for stuff.
26. Having an "it's just" mentality that allows little expenses to quickly add up.
27. Ignoring bank fees. Especially overdraft fees. They add up real fast
28. Not using credit cards early enough.
29. Not using credit cards properly.
30. Not regularly checking credit report.
31. Not setting financial boundaries with loved ones.
32. Not paying tithes.
33. Ignoring financial compatibility in relationships.
34. Being afraid to be "that person" who says no to spending money because all of your friends are doing it.

# FINANCIAL TOOLS AND RESOURCES

Special worksheets for each chapter can be found online. Check the 20-Something & Rich Facebook Group. Here are some other resources that can help you with your finances!

- Mint.com
- Creditkarma.com
- Tuition.io
- Readyforzero.com
- Bankrate.com
- Personalcapital.com
- Powerwallet.com
- Inexfinance.com
- Jemstep.com

Check out these online sites to see what financial resource are best for you. These sites do everything from helping you manage your budget to recommending what you should do with your IRA. Don't neglect this opportunity to use technology to make your life easier.

CPSIA information can be obtained
at www.ICGtesting.com
Printed in the USA
BVOW06s0953221217
503398BV00038B/824/P